Clear as Mud

Clear as Mud

Wendy Mae Crichton

First Edition
Copyright
March 2019

MacDonald Publishing

London, Canada
www.MacDonaldPost.com

Clear as Mud
Copyright © 2019
MacDonald Publishing
London, Canada
ISBN: 978-1-7753271-4-1 (pbk)

Unless specified, all Scripture quotations are taken from the King James Bible.

All rights reserved. No part of this publication may be reproduced, stored in a retrieval system, or transmitted in any form or by any means—electronic, mechanical, photocopy, recording, or otherwise—without written permission of the publisher, except for brief quotations in printed reviews.

Printed in Canada and USA

This book is dedicated to the most important people in my life, my children, their spouses and all my grandchildren. Being a Christian is my priority and being my children's mother and grandmother has been a gift from God. God is so important in our lives and I pray often for my family and friends.

"Therefore if any man be in Christ, he is a new creature: old things are passed away; behold, all things are become new."

2 Corinthians 5:17

Clear as Mud

Preface xi
Poetry 1
   Christmas Snow 1
   More Precious than Gold 1Peter 1:7 2
   Treasures 3
   The Whisper 4
   Curtis and Annmarie 5
   July 18, 2009 6
   Tadpoles 7
   Reflections 8
   Console Me 9
   The Loss 10
   Christmas Day 12
   Listening 13
   Sweet Dreams 14
   Little 15
   Our Elderly 16
   The Root 17
   Threw Out the Life Line 18
   Don't Forget Me 19
   Did You Notice? 20
   Mothers Love 21
   Follow the Master 22
   Mercy 23
   Kristen 24
   Our Baby Girl 26

That Day Came	27
Six yellow Roses	28
Family	29
Emily and Matthew	30
It's Funny	31
Irreplaceable	32
The Visit	33
The Moon	34
Stayed	35
Away	36
Come	37
My Mattie Boy	38
Judgments	39
Journey	40
Missing You Wendy	41
Blue	42
Rhonda, the Salon	43
Wendy, My Little Girl	44
… EVER …	45
Tracey	46
Lois	47
Freda	48
Battles	49
The House	50
The Nursery	51
Carolynn Chloe Belle Mardis	52
Reassurance	53
Passion	54

Princess	55
Wild Heart	56
Sassafras Moonbeams	57
Tomorrow	58
One Tear after Another	59
It's only my Poor Heart	60
My Knight	61
Long Blonde Hair	62
Cologne	63
Old Records	64
Dragons	65
Love has many Stories	66
My Little Girl	67
Our Teacher	68
Walk Away	69
Oh to be	70
Old Clothes	71
Puppies	72
Mother	73
Suntan lines	74
Anne & Bob	75
The Lesson	76
Never Known	77
Foresee	78

Preface

As a young girl, our Lord Jesus Christ knew of the disasters to come in my life, and He would carry me through those difficult times. I desperately needed Him. God's mighty hands are at work in my life. He would mend my broken heart, dry my tears and rebuild my life, so I could continue to serve Him. When time looked its bleakest God gave me his love freely. Handling my situations in life I've had to leave the future up to Him. My poems are great comfort to me and I pray that they touch and inspire those that read my book. Life's struggles, pain, unfulfillment, frustrations, kindness, encouragements and support, these have helped me to put words to my thoughts and to be bold in my writings.

Wendy Mae Crichton

Christmas Snow

Here I stand shivering in the cold
Watching the snow dance on
a snowy December day.
Winter winds are blowing in our small town.
and the Christmas lights, they sparkle
But to me they seem to lack a certain glow.
It's you I miss
that's the emptiness in me.
I can still see my children playing in the Christmas snow,
they'd laugh and play and make snow angels.
Everything seems to remind me.
As I stand here shivering in the cold
Its frozen tears I cry, as I reminisce
It's you I miss the most, not presents or turkeys that are stuffed.
You're a mother now and how that
will bring new meanings to your Christmas.
Then you will know how much you truly meant to me
Christmas comes once a year, maybe someday you'll come back to me.
Stars of wonder, shimmering in the snow
I wish this for me on Christmas day.
A gift.
A hug of warmth from my children I pray.

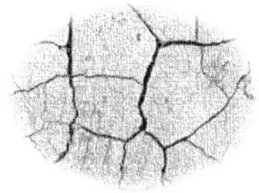

More Precious than Gold 1Peter 1:7

A Kiss
In my quietness, my time is still. I gaze at the gift my daughter has given. Just a little girl, but she loves her mom. I can't stop the tears, what a tender heart my little girls been given. As I remember it started in the month of September.
Mom, if you buy a chocolate bar can I have the paper, and a piece! What for I'd say? I'm saving it and she'd be on her way. She asked her brothers to do the same, save them for me don't through them away. They would reply, aren't girl strange, but they'd save them for her. Dad, don't forget, I'm saving them, yes dear I remember as he continued watching TV.
My dear what are you doing, mom I'm making something and she would scamper upstairs. Well don't make a mess and don't use all my tape. No mom, I won't, just need a little bit.
December is busy and you're always rushed, places to go, things to buy, people to see and yes, the Christmas tree. Children are excited; our Church play was a success. The day is for Jesus for he is the perfect gift. Christmas morn is here the bells will all ring. Let's bring in the morning with Christmas cheer and sing. We read the Christmas story to open up our hearts and now the gifts are given,
each one taken apart.
My daughter she is so happy but she sits to wait for me,
but her smile is so precious as she hands her gift to me.
Mommy, I hope you like it I made it just for you. The family stopped to watch for they are curious too. I kissed her little face than opened up the gift. Tears of love began to flow, for she had covered a little box completely with the gold wrappers from the chocolate bars. It was just beautiful a golden jewelry box, and on the top was written in gold glitter glue:
Merry Christmas, and inside a kiss is for you.
A child's labor of love.
Merry Christmas

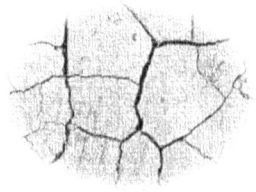

Treasures

Wendy and Jerry
Our day has come and God is with us.
I delight in God's goodness and know his goodness will be in us.
This day
I will marry my friend.
The one I laugh with,
Live for, dream of and love.
Our day has come and I will trust that you have my best interests at heart.
I will cling to your promise,
You'll be with me and love me.
My heart is at peace knowing that you haven't limited yourself to the visible,
My mind has been on nothing else but our dreams of the life together we'll have.
I feel the passion in your touch and I know I'm loved.
The first time I held you I knew I could love you for the rest of our lives.
God will be at the head of our new life together
And continue to be there in our future.
I look back at our past memories with amazement;
God's leading has brought us together
and how I anticipate all the things that we will do together.
Evening has come and my soul is quiet and as we turn off the light,
tonight we will remember the light and love that burns within us.
Lord, help us to be the man and woman that you want us to be,
Help us to shift our focus from me to us.
Our life's trials and adventures will now be shared together.
Jesus said our heart will be where our treasure is, so God first,
And with a delicate whisper my love tells me......
My treasure is you.

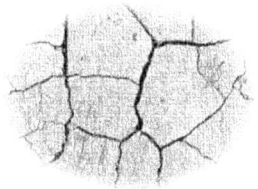

The Whisper

In a low whisper, he said to me,
I love you
As we looked at each other
Face to face.
In the clutch of loves embrace
There we stood,
Before God, we said our vows
and told each other we'll be true.
Oh how our love has been a prelude
that never dies.
Still holding hands,
walking side by side.
I've never grown tired of his sweet, sweet whisper,
I love you
Oh how you've always set my heart on fire.
Our love song
has played for years,
face to face,
hand in hand,
my heart still over flows.
We whisper together
I love you
Loves sweet spirit has touched us and lasted our life time.
Memories, as I reminisce we have been so blessed.
I whisper softly in his ear,
can you hear me,
I love you
As I hold his hand
I quiver at the thought,
He'll not be beside me for a while.
His eyes have closed but I know God is near,
How do I face tomorrow, without him?
Now in a quiet voice
I hear the whisper of Jesus,
I love you.
As I sit here so close beside him, face to face and hold his hands
And watched his life's fire, his soul quietly and peacefully disappear.
I whispered
Through my inconsolable tears
I love you.

Curtis and Annmarie

- **C** Continually seeking God's wisdom
  - **A** And we will honor God so our marriage is honorable in the sight of God.
- **U** United we will be and our unfolding Love, with your quiet spirit and our
  - **N** New hearts and
  - **N** New spirit will be one flesh.
- **R** Remembering roses and Moonlight and
  - **M** Memories.
- **T** Trust even in the midst of failure.
  - **A** Always obey god.
- **I** Intimacy involves personal interaction, commitment and caring to continue lasting
  - **R** Romance.
- **S** Slow to anger and quick to praise, be soft and sensitive, strong and
  - **I** In
  - **E** Every season of your lives, Pray.

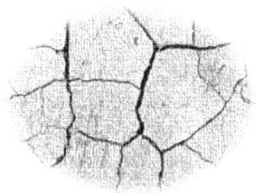

July 18, 2009

I, Andrew
On bended knee
have taken her hands
and looked deep into her eyes,
with a nervous voice
but the strength of a man
I've asked her,
Christina.
Will you Marry Me
and change your name
so you are only mine?
Our passion is strong
and our dreams
we'll build together.
God knows our hearts
and we'll count our blessings.
Two golden bands
circles of endless Love
Two hearts that
have come together
to share a lifetime of love.

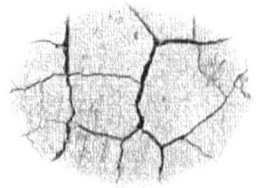

Tadpoles

I've reached a certain milestone in my life,
I thought people wouldn't influence me at all, I was so wrong.
I've lived and tried life, married, had children.
I've done some pretty crazy things, laughed a lot,
loved lots of people and have great lifelong soul mates.
Great dogs that became part of the family, loyal right to the end.
Then came the day when I saw little faces, my grandchildren, life has new meaning.
I still find it so hard to believe how they've stirred my heart and completed my soul
When they call me Grandma Frog.
I wanted to be that grandma who would tend to her blossoms.
Weather in actual flowers or in acts of kindness and love.
The first time I held them I knew I would love them for the rest of my life.
But each day is anew, whether it brings joy or sadness, it's a new day.
So today I watched my son drive right past my house again and all that I can think of
Is why and I start to cry, I've lost my son.
He's still alive but my soul is in morning.
Words have been said but salted with angry questions and I am reaping the crippling effects of bitterness.
Life is so hard, God messages are so clear and controlled so why do I constantly
feel like I am in a state of confusion and full of problems.
Lord whisper to me your Spirit controlled wisdom, don't let me be robbed of your kindness.
My body is so full of sorrow. It feels like I'm melting like wax.
There goes my grandchildren, my small taste of heaven, loneliness wears many
different faces and as I focus on yesterday and cry all day today.
I know God is there for me tomorrow but my joy is overshadowed by the loss of their little faces.
Grandma Frogs little Tadpoles.

Reflections

It's a beautiful cold winter evening for a walk near the woods. The moonlight shimmers
through the pine trees. I catch the scent, their sweet smell makes my mind wonder through
memories. I ponder over the challenges God has given me and burdens laid on my heart, I know
God is in control and he is with me,
My most difficult journey is going back to the places where I feel I have failed. Yet I don't
want regrets to become a major past time.
This marriage of ours, I feel is taking the life out of me. It's so hard to live with a man
when the love you give is never given back.
Lord help me to enjoy my walk, don't let old memories talk to me. I know the past is always nearby.
The chill of reality goes directly to my bones and the only thing let between us is distance. I'm not crying any more. There are certain passions one only learns threw pain.
Love is like the wind it never reveals its destiny.
This walk is ending and now as I sit in the comfort of my home,
I felt my heart strangely warmed, God's love for me.
I tried to understand, when did my dreams changed. I can't believe I've watched my life disappear. Age should not be our enemy, there are some that don't have the privilege.
Lord, forgive me for my molecule of faith, sometimes it's so hard to see. I know you love me and I'm well loved. My strength in you I need when I'm weak, there is an emptiness that I need filled.
A leaf in the wind is helpless, be with me Lord give me courage to set aside the hurts and rejoice.
Now there's darkness in the night and frost on the window and a reflection of me alone on the glass.

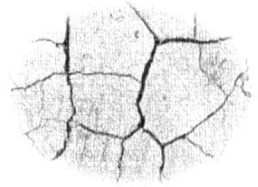

Console Me

Driving to the airport
not a word was spoken
I couldn't say anything.
There were a million thoughts
racing through my mind.
I should have been telling her
how much I loved her
and how much I'll kiss her
but I just couldn't.
This was her time to live
every moment her way.
I held her hand
I wanted time to stop.
How am I ever going to function without her?
Is my life really continuing?
I hugged and kissed her,
held her face in my hands.
Why do I have to let you go?
Mom we can do this?
I watched them both,
My daughter and her new husband
until they faded away.
My strength was gone my heart sunk.
A stranger offered me a chair.
She tried to console me,
but I was deaf to her kind words.
Knowing I wouldn't see my little girl again
for such a long time and miles between us.
Will she keep me in her heart?
She was my world. God's gift.
Tonight I will cry myself to sleep
with a heart so inconsolable.
How I hate this chapter in my life
the journey makes me so weary.
My soul is in need of God's love.
Hear me calling.

The Loss

All my life I wanted a home, a home that was truly mine. I remember saying to friends and family that I wanted them to be comfortable here, at peace, to feel that they were maybe walking into Grandma's house, a home of love and memories. When you looked around the rooms and see each individual piece of furniture carefully placed and refinished, each had its own little story.

I tried so hard, I gave all I could to my marriage and my children. I loved them and they were happy and full of fun. We would read, play games, make crafts, bake and have sleepovers. I thought I was making this house our home. A home that might have been and could have been our dreams.

We would sit often in the living room by the big front window and watch storms come in and light up the sky with terrific sounds of thunder. Birthdays and holidays I tried to make them big and individual so my children could have wonderful childhood memories. We worked together, cut grass and gardened, had backyard bonfires, just sitting and watching the stars and of course the dogs and cats and bunnies to care for. Our lives where so busy and as my children go older life just got more exciting. I did make my old hours, God was directing and protecting us.

I've been told so many times, my home, it's just brick, mortar and wood, well, I do believe their wrong. There are so many reasons why a house is called The Family Home. The main reason is life, our life has been lived there. This home I loved is now simply a house, thirty years or more from now some other women might stand as I did dozens of times in the wonderful l living room saying "I'll never leave here".

God had different plans for me or maybe I was just in a losing battle. My home is now empty, it has strange echoes of silence. My children's hearts grew and blossomed here and I wanted so much for my grandchildren to run through my home and yard and pick flowers in Grandmas gardens. I feel so alone in this, like we never existed. Can know one else feel my pain or see my loss, did it even matter.

The lights are out, the doors are all closed, my hand on the doorknob, I'm lingering just a little longer. Tears fill my eyes, my shoulders rise and fall, gasps catch in my chest and my hands hang limp. After a few minutes, I feel the calm that comes from acknowledging what's been lost. There was so much more living I wanted to do here, my children played in this backyard. I'm holding on to our memories, they will always come with me. Going home now has a whole different meaning. I have to forget all I used to be, time just slipped away and it has a way of separating whims from needs.

God give me courage to set aside hurts and rejoice, are failures forgivable.

It's not my home anymore.

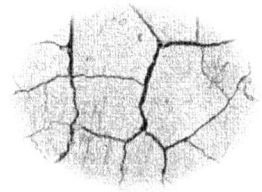

Christmas Day

This Christmas Eve will be just a little different than the rest. Thankfully the Christ Child will always be in our hearts and lives. It's just that now my heart is slower and many years have crept on pasted. Life's windows are now closing and my memories are all I have left. Children what a blessing you truly have been to me, treasures when life was full of high sea storms. My God and you children were my anchors when I was tossed around. God always knew I needed you, no matter what stage of life I was at. Those memories have always refreshed my mind even now when I take my last breaths.

Remembering the dandelions you picked for me. The colored rocks that would end up in the wash and the pennies and marbles too. Ice cream that always dripped but we would sit, laugh and lick. Tobogganing was just as fun, sometimes we'd go at night. My children and their friends would pile in the back of that old pick-up truck on a crisp dark night till all were cold and freezing. Fighting over who would go down the hill and get the sleighs left at the bottom of the hill before it was time to go home.

School projects and class trips, who would ever think I'd miss those days, I can't forget the Christmas plays at school and Church. The songs you sang and the verses learned, nothing filled my heart more with such joy. I have kept a few toys, books and some of your little clothes. Many times I have walked past them and they are just collecting dust. How was I to know the years would pass so quickly, tears and tears, oh how I want that time back. Bedtime stories, teddies and kisses. Children grow up and each is so precious. Weeks, month and years a life time full of God's gifts and not realizing it. I remember now when a dear friend said to me on one of those days when a storm was might high. My friend would say do not wish your life away, it will never come again, so enjoy.

Christmas gifts are always given to those of us truly living year by year, month by week, and day and night with each bedtime kiss. Now here I lay on my last Christmas day and praise God for those memories. My children whisper softly and squeeze my hand tight, "Mommy I love you!" I reply, "I am still here, my sight is clearer than ever and I can hear your crying. I love you all so much, I am weak and God's precious gift of life is dying. It's Christmas day but I cannot stay, my Lord is waiting. You have God's gifts, so use them wisely, love life and those within it, with lots of bedtime stories and little ones hugs and kisses. Remember this always, I Love you, "Merry Christmas my children!

Listening

Tattered and torn are
the pages of my old Bible.
There are days I'd read
through my tears.
Touching the past,
as I rub my fingers
across the pages.
My pain I can't escape,
It's hard to hide.
Maybe I'm reading it all wrong.
I'm just over come with grief.
Lord, help my heart to sing again
remove the shadows from my eyes.
My Bible is still open
and my mind still desires, The Word.
Lord I'm sure you know I wasn't listening,
My heart was blind.

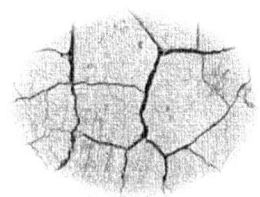

Sweet Dreams

Watching the sunrise it takes my breath away, as we drive down that dusty road.
Not a drop of rain in sight, the heat is blistering. The kind of heat that only appeals to corn growing in fields basking in the sun. Then I see my daughter's house, pale yellow and an aura of calmness around it. You almost get swallowed up in the silence.
Off in the distance though, you can hear the soft whistle of a train and see yellow butterflies having fun in the sun.
She's happy here and there's great peace in my soul when she can wake up and know there's family who love her. God has given her a baby son a precious gift wrapped in a soft blanket.
Grandma's come to visit, to see her grandson. He falls asleep so quickly I can hardly see his blue eyes. She is a good mom, her mothering arms are made of tenderness and her baby sleeps soundly in them. Gazing at him trying to determine whose side of the family is responsible for those little ears and button nose.
I can hardly wait till he can run to Grandma for a hug. For now we're apart, we've said goodbye, I just broke down and cried, and again my world is tore apart.
Sweet dreams baby boy, I'll send my love for you on angel wings. Each night I know God hears our prayers where ever we are.
I just get tired of wiping tears of my cheeks,
Sweet dreams.

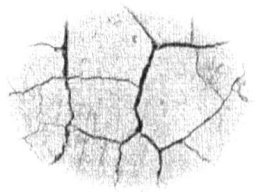

Little

I knew the day would come, excitement, fear and fulfillment, my little girl was going off to college. Giving your child up to do the Lord's will is a good thing. It's just hard on the heart.
When we drove her up there we were all talking about nonsensical things. Me avoiding the obvious, she's leaving me. It's taken a lifetime to realize to in joy every minute slowly so you can savor the moment.
Over years I've felt the loss that comes from the death of family and friends and I know the hurts of family struggles and I've had pains and fears. But when I left my daughter at someone else' doorstep and drove away my heart just stopped. This kind of sadness I've never known just breathing was difficult, a heaviness that wouldn't lift and a fountain of tears I couldn't control.
Time has silently stolen her from me. I remember hanging on to my wee baby girl and being so thankful to have her. Now holding her face and saying goodbye. Lord make me brave, please let this moment linger.
I realize if you live in the past it cost you your future, but today tears still fall. She'd written me a letter, left it at home so I would get it. Here I am out on the swing a beautiful day reading her letter again and again crying inconsolably. My sons knew my pain, they gave me gifts and flowers but their tender hearts and hugs just made me cry.
I am so loved by this family of mine.
God has surely blessed me with tender hearts that cry.
Little, I miss the beauty of your presence. I miss you my little girl.

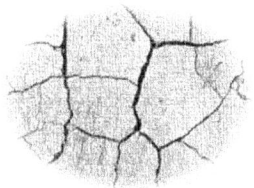

Our Elderly

There are some people at our Church
That cares a lot about me.
Even though I don't
Really know them very well, I defiantly can see
Their always around
To lend a hand
Or extend a hand of curtsey.
I've seen them sad on rare occasions
But mostly their happy
And glad to see us teens.
I've witnessed their hard work
And their pain of some disappointments.
I can see their friendships and their loyal devotions.
I know, God is at work in their lives
And His strength gives them victories.
I've seen them all in bended knee
And I'm sure, they prayed for me.
As I grow and time gets hold of me
And he takes through many victories
I know our Lord is there for me
Just as He's been with our Beloved Elderly

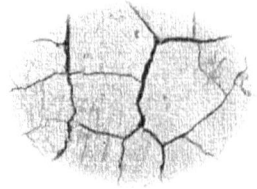

The Root

The root of a
Family tree
Begins with the
Love
Of two hearts
One
Branch,
Fertilized
With
Time.

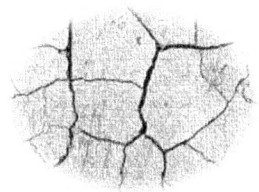

Threw Out the Life Line

In my dreams I can bid farewell to everyone.
I can sail through waves of troubles
and drift with the wind.
I can go to open waters and lighten up my load of sin.
My Jesus he's always there for me
but this time he asked,
Where's your friends.
Now I've sunk into the clay and I've learned the hard way.
As I gazed upon the Son.
He made me realize I'd forgotten the ones I love.
By yourself it's not a good thing.
He knows family disappointment, but they need you.
Friends they'll disappoint you too
but they'll sail with you to the end.
so gather them up and sail away
Sail till you hit shores of white sand.
With bare feet you'll walk a while
and share God's plan.
Now let the moon follow you home
and drift there with the wind.
Wake up on a different shore
and don't forget your friend.

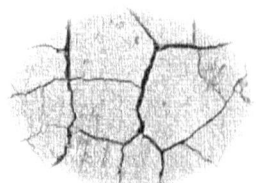

Don't Forget Me

I've met a new bunch of girls
that reminded me of me.
I was lost; I forgot who I was,
I was at the end of that mad race.
Where I stood with my head
Down, holding my face.
Pure exhaustion and the pain of helplessness,
Tears of extreme loneliness.
those girls knew where I was
because they've been there too.
Don't forget me, I cried!
Then they held out their hands then waved
and yelled, you've made it there.
There so much more
you've reached the other side.
Try not to cry, dry your eyes.
Those girls they helped me,
They helped me to see.
That reflection in the mirror,
it really is me.
A beautiful woman, inside and out
those girls are amazing, lifelong friends, without a doubt.

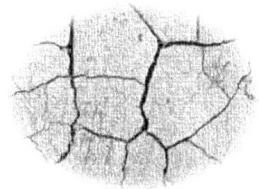

Did You Notice?

Far too long my head's been down……
Did anyone notice my eyes were blackened?
Far too long I've been forgotten.
Did anyone see the bruises I'd gotten?
Far too long I've cried night after night.
Did anyone see the tears that had fallen?
Far too long I said I was Sorry.
Did anyone hear me cries for help?
Far too long I laid there bruised and broken.
Did anyone notice this women's life was taken?

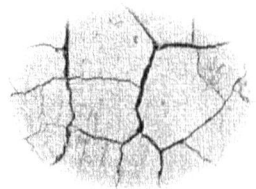

Mothers Love

It's now thirty years that's past and I still can't find it.
Her perfume, soap or powder a scent that can't be found.
Youth has a way of hiding thing that are important for later.
Although it's finding something that's not lost just misplaced in memories
and years of life.
Now just busy getting older and full of responsibilities, time just went by.
Though little things arouse that sense of loss now more so then ever before.
I try to let those moments linger.
It was hard for me as a little girl to understand.
Why did it have to end with a slow ride in a hearse? My mom was gone.
Being a mother now myself, the hurt she must have been
going through leaving her children.
Seeing their faces full of tears and the uncertainty in their eyes and nothing
could she do?
Thinking only of what she could and should have done before her time.
I'm sure it was comforting to knowing that she was so well loved.
It's taken a while but I've found
that scent, it's a mother's Love.

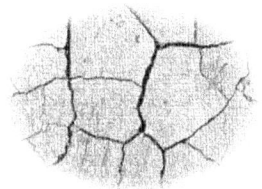

Follow the Master

There are mountains of stress in our lives but mountains are meant to be climbed.
To the top and over, from a distance mountains make a beautiful landscape.
Life is cause and effect and every trial I face in my life I want it to lead me to God's Grace. I want to be led by the unseen Spirit.
The past is always nearby to step back and look at. My troubles I pray that God will give me endurance. I might lose the battle but I am not defeated. I know God is in control.
Jesus unlaced the sandals of his disciples and put their feet gently in the basin just hours before his own death. Jesus wanted his disciples to know how much he loved them. Jesus did not just remove dirt, he was removing doubt.
Jesus hands and feet were pierced and lifeless. He knew the future of his disciple's feet and that they were going to abandon him.
By morning their heads will hang in shame and look down at their own feet in disgrace. How amazing that the disciples were forgiven their sins before they were even committed. They were given mercy before they even asked for it.
What Jesus did for them he'll do for us? He'll cleanse us by the blood of Jesus Christ and walk with us always.
He still washes feet.

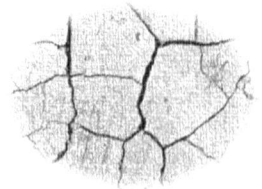

Mercy

Soon today will be over and the Lord will lay His blanket of darkness upon us.
How can I erase the memory of this day?
My son, walking right past me, I'm a stranger in his eyes.
No one seems to need me like they did before.
Our home was a part of me, now a memory.
My children's hand prints I've washed them off the walls and their crayons, they're all lost.
The yard is now still.
Time silently steals.
Defeat is on my body and time has put grey in my hair, that wasn't there before.
My life is littered with broken hearts.
I'm still crying tears from a long time ago, life is so confusing.
Time has hurt me long enough today.
Your silence says more than anything.
As a little boy you would say,
"I will always love you Mommy."
I guess today was the end of always.
I don't want others to catch me crying or see the hurt in my eyes.
My brokenness might start to heal when Satan takes his hands off me.
Lord, I don't know what to say but I know I need a crumb of your mercy today.
Lord, I'm not worthy of your whole loaf of bread.
I'm crying for a crumb to fall my way.

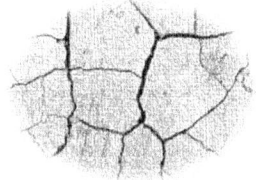

Kristen

The gift of our little girl Kristen has blessed our lives forever.
So many times I have to catch my breath when someone mentions her name.
My body shivers at the thought of our loss. I am so full of sorrow, I feel I could melt like wax.
Lord whisper to me your controlled wisdom and love, don't let me be robbed of your kindness.
So many times I just want to breakdown and cry. I know God hears my heart crying.
My little girl stirred my heart and completed my soul, she was a small piece of heaven.
A year has gone by, I haven't forgotten how beautiful she was.
Lord give me the courage to carry on and gather my yesterdays like a bouquet full of warm memories.
What a privilege we've been given to have had her in our lives.
There is nothing on earth that can replace that need in my heart.
Memories of dancing timeless steps around the living room.
Party dresses, beauty pagans, rainbows and her endeavor to play the piano.
Her childhood giggles are engraved on my heart, for an instant the tick of time relents.
Family photo albums are now my treasures with her and her two brothers
And you can see her love for animals, we were so Blessed.
Rubbing my fingers across those pages of her past,
memories of lullabies and precious baby pictures.
How I'm drawn in by her green eyes and the sweetness of her smile.
Oh my little girl there was so much more we hadn't done.
We had so many fun filled days with her and I,
as we would sometimes just laughed till we cried.
Oh how I still want to kiss all her tears away.
There's a window at our Church were you liked to sit and just stare out at the sky.
Like you were having long conversations with God
and you would play with the tip of your pencil.
I wasn't prepared when she went off to kindergarten and
I'm not prepared now for my broken heart.
There's an unnatural silence now in our home.
I get on my knees and through my tears I read Gods comforting words
In my tattered and torn pages of my Bible.

But as Kristen's mom how I'd love to tell her once more how much she meant to me and I want to tell her over and over again how much I love her and want to hold her in my arms.
But God has called her home and He is now holding her in his arms.
As I walk to where you now rest and I listen to the birds sweetly singing in a nearby tree.
Yellow roses I have picked for you, Kristen and placed them here on the ground,
Now Crowns of Glory you'll now have to place at Jesus feet.

Kristen Elizabeth Shepard
May 01, 1997, July 15, 2014

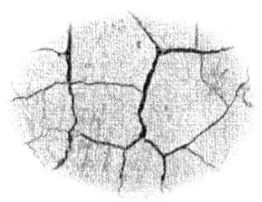

Our Baby Girl.

Lily

The yard is still, but I'll tend to the garden
my grandson once said to me,
Grandma, do you still have flowers.
As I pull the weeds from my garden nourishing the flowers of life
the rewards are in every blossom.
Standing here on the front porch at my daughter's home
the moments linger with anticipation of a new born baby.
I haven't forgotten how beautiful my daughter was as a new born babe.
Memories that never fade, my legacy.
With children of her own,
now she'll understand how much she meant to me.
The phone rings and I'm told, "It's a girl".
The very first time I saw her I knew I could love her for the rest of my life.
It's funny how such a small thing can change our lives, forever.
The pink little bundle, a cocoon of emotions, a cradle of hope in Christ.
Grandma helps to calm her cries and paces the floors and hush her to sleep.
As I held her small graceful hand, I couldn't help but think,
maybe she'll play the piano just like her mommy.
There are lullabies and pictures taken and kisses given, all while you sleep.
Your little ears can now handle the soft whispers of big brother and his kisses.
I'd sit and rock baby at night and all I could see was the moonlight.
Perhaps it was the wind that spoke or the stars could see
The heart to heart talks between her and me.
There may be generations that divide us but love unites this baby and me.
It's time for Grandma to leave.
I watch you all and we cry till you fade away, waving goodbye.
Dear Lord please wave your mercy over us and calm our hearts
because of the miles between us.
Marigolds of yellow with sunny tomorrows and a new grandbaby named Lily.
I can't wait for the day she'll blossom and play
and plant her own seeds of life for tomorrow.
In her journey I'll help scatter her seeds
So she'll yield fields of beautiful flowers in fields of her life
and harvest rewards in every blossom which started in
Grandma's Garden.
My little flower, Lily Mae Anne Mardis

That Day Came

How does one say goodbye to their child? The days are winding down and I don't want to see what my heart already knows.
So many days I just break down and cry. She's leaving me and time keeps slipping by. Life has no mercy, it has no feelings, and it just tears your heart apart. I want my heart to stand still, frozen so reality doesn't come to light. I quiver at the thought of letting her go. These precious last days that I spend with my daughter they're days that I wish would last forever. Perhaps it's the winds that softly speak to me, hold your eyes and tears on the memories, so she can leave with hers.
As a little girl she wanted a pony and many times she would bring me handfuls of dandelion bouquets. As a teenager bare feet always on the dashboard. Now a young man has stolen her heart and everyone can see that she loves him. Just like the wind it never reveals its destiny, so now her journey is beginning.
I know this has to happen but it's not easy. Every muscle in my body screams, NO! Lord, make me brave for this is insurmountable without you, help me to hide my pain. I'm trying not to limit my vision. I want to choose eyes that see the unseen and beyond but I'm only human. I want to hide in God's power. Can't I hold onto her for just a little longer, can't this moment linger?
I have to let her go. God is watching and I know he sees the hurt in me and knows a mother's love, her hopes and legacy.
For her my prayers are asked, because of her my life has been well lived, because of her I've been blessed, because of her I've been given just a small taste of God" great love.
That lasts forever.

August 2011

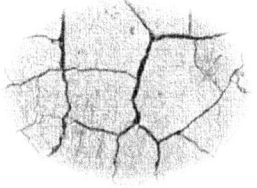

Six yellow Roses

It's been so common for us to gather at moms, it's not the same with her gone.
This house is not her home anymore.
God has called her.
With sorrow and tears we'll turn off the lights and close the doors.
Remembering more pleasurable times.
Our memories are so sweet, that's the way it should be.
Her life wasn't easy, but how hard she tried.
She loved the yellow roses planted in her garden
and in her garden of life she had six beautiful rosebuds her daughters.
It's quiet now where she sleeps
but how I'd love to tell her one more time that I love her.
I want to walk with her in the garden, but she doesn't live there anymore.
I'll pick the yellow roses for her
and in my garden of life.
I'll tend to the rose buds
and watch them bloom in memory of you, mom.

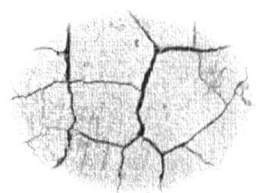

Family

As the moon light dazzles and gives a light glow.
I remember my family, seems so long ago.
We would talk and share dreams, like most families do.
Troubles would come, the phone would ring.
We'd talk forever, about silly things.
Troubles would be forgotten, our laughs change the day.
It's funny how things happen as we get older,
people just walk away.
Years turn families into strangers and differences into walls.
Troubles turn in arguments, the phone just doesn't ring.
Our laugh is now silent, troubles just linger on.
Our silence becomes distance.
As adults we've forgotten how to play. Adults hold grudges
and money can sometimes divide.
So the family is forgotten.
as I gaze in the moonlight,
it seems just like yesterday.

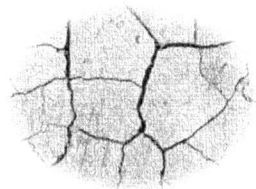

Emily and Matthew

The great pleasure in one's life is the search after the heart.
God's leading has brought us together.
Remembering red roses, moonlight and memories along our journey,
that's what brings us to this day.
Our wedding rings are on display and every minute is important.
After this day we'll never face the world alone.
Today is our day.
Just as every journey has one step, ours now begins.
We'll hold hands with the one who is the giver of life.
The Lord Jesus Christ
and know that our journey is Blessed.
Loves sweet spirit has touched us and it will last our life time.
We stand before God and say our Vows
Face to face
and look into each other's eyes,
In the clutch of loves embrace.
Our hearts will be at peace knowing God is with us.
She told me her feelings and she knows how much she means to me.
United we will be and our unfolding love,
with God's quiet Spirit, our new hearts will be one flesh.
We'll have romance and enchanted evenings,
We'll be quick to praise, but slow to anger.
We'll be soft, sensitive and strong.
Remembering silence says more than anything.
We'll never doubt our love
But we will always dance in the moonlight.
We'll nestle in each other arms and swim the sea of passion, side by side.
I pray her heart will flutter each time she feels my breath on her cheek.
As I whisper in her ear,
sweet dreams my wife,
I love you.

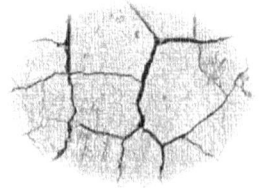

It's Funny

He's just a young man so in love with this young lady.
They laugh and dream, hold hands and have long walks and talks in the park.
Kicking stones, making plans for another day.
Biking on hot summer days,
they are just enjoying the length and warmth of each day.
Soon enough autumn is here and they must part for another year.
No easy way to say goodbye.
I'll close my eyes she says so I can't watch you leave
and he'll wait till she's gone before he sheds a tear.
He tells her though, she's his only need and she replies
my heart drives me back to you.
It's funny how love will make a way.
So they smile and say good bye
I love you

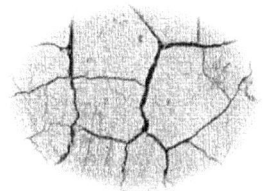

Irreplaceable

Hold me Daddy
Love me,
For life is taking
Me day by day.
I'm growing
Find the time, daddy.
Be with me.
Precious moments
with you and I'm your little boy.
Time is an immeasurable gift, life.
Just once this day is here.
I love you daddy.

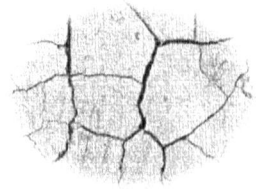

The Visit

I have a life time of memories
and many photo albums of picture.
Memories I try to secure them in my heart.
Children, their love
their sweet innocence's.
Will they ever know how much I love them?
It's never enough,
my time with them,
Its way too short.
This is surely something
I've never faced before.
Now a Grandmother
What a blessing for them to come and have a visit.
New memories and a lot more pictures.

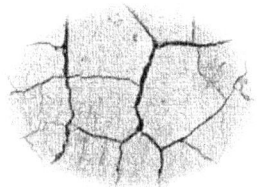

The Moon

We've longed for these days, time to gather memories.
Hot, hot days
Sunny Sundays afternoons.
With two scoops of ice-cream
and sharing it with you
right to the last bite.
Bare feet on the dash board
talking about everything and nothing.
Does my heart really understand?
What love really is?
We walked at the beach
held each other tight,
listened to the waves.
Then let the moon follow us home.
It's hard not to watch you
and to love the little things you do.
Now lunch with the family
and friends and the baby he's the entertainer too. Time goes so quickly.
I'm not ready to say goodbye.
We must hold on to the moments until another night.
Softly kiss my tears away.
I know I lost my heart on these kinds of days
and I realize how much I miss you.
Especially on starry nights
watching the harvest moon.

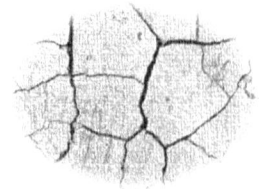

Stayed

Thirty years of tears
Don't wash off cleanly,
They stain the inside of one's heart.
I stayed for the children,
I stayed because I was lost and didn't know what to do.
I stayed because
of responsibilities and the love I thought I knew.
I stayed because
I was afraid.
Hated and loved,
worthless and needed
confused and assurance,
husband and my children.
I didn't realize I was lost and not needed.

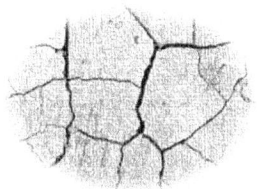

Away

Today I saw tears fall
that broke my heart.
You're just a little boy
and I'm scared for you,
Life shouldn't be that way.
Why do people
Just walk away.
There's anger there
Can't you see?
Sweet boy
Your probably only three
and love just walks away.

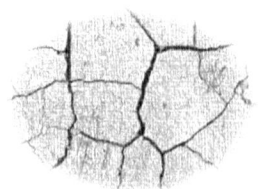

Come

He wiped the tears
from his cheeks
and turned his head
so I couldn't see.
But I seen more than what I wanted to
and my heart went
out to get you.
Come to Grandma
my precious boy
for love, hugs and kisses.

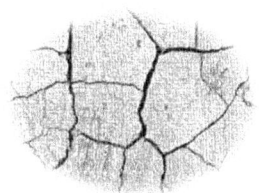

My Mattie Boy

That first night when I knew you wouldn't be
coming home, that was a lonely, lonely tearful night.
My baby boy now a grown young man, off to college.
Goodbyes are not easy for a mother to do, your heart
Seems to get stretched to the bursting point.
Saying goodbye takes every bit of energy out of me.
My heart feels like it is lying lifeless on the floor.
Getting you ready to go I was determined not to cry.
I tried to stay busy getting your things together and packing
up your car but you can't hide tears.
Kissing your face and waving goodbye, I sure liked it
better when you were only five and just taking that
big step going into kindergarten.
I guess I just forgot you were getting older.
I was enjoying our life time together so much and now it seemed so brief.
The day you came into my life as a new baby it was cold and snowing.
Today we say goodbye and it is cold and snowing.
Now you are going into a world far beyond our little snow filled back yard.
I closed the glass door and then watched you give your doggie a big hug and
a loving pat on his head.
It just made my tears fall even more.
I thank God for giving me such a tenderhearted son.
My hands pressed against that cold glass door as my son drives away.
Lord being a mother is so hard,
give me the strength for another day, for today I have none.
Lord continue to guide and protect him.
Keep your loving arms around him.
Heavenly father, he will need you more than ever because his mom's too far
away.

Xoxoxoxooooooooooooooooooxoxoxo

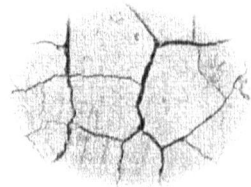

Judgments

I watched my son and his young family drive past my house again today. All that I could think of is why? And then cry.
I feel like I'm in a state of morning, facing challenges that outweigh my strengths. Life is hard and too many times tears flow. My first grandchildren and I thought I was a part of their young lives. I've gotten my share of scares in my life but being distant from my family is heart wrenching.
Words get spoken things are assumed and things get spoken salted with angry questions. God is in control but my life always seems full of problems. Passing judgments on my life knowing only fragments of situations how can you judge me without a broader picture.
Time heals, apologies can be given but are they.

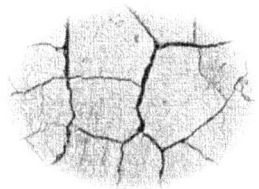

Journey

It's funny how different situations in your life mould you.
I struggle with getting older not the age but ability.
Winter is my favorite time of the year.
The crisp cold air, fluffy snow.
I still would like to be able
to climb to the top of that mound of snow.
Slide down and then go right back up to the top and slide down again,
screaming and laughing with a happy heart.
Life has so many seasons and I have found getting older is the most difficult.
Youth seems to have no limits.
Looking threw that frosted window as I sit motionless in this chair.
The heart is willing but the body cannot
my window of life has changed again.
I must take the hand of the one that is the giver of life.
The Lord Jesus Christ
and know that my new journey will soon be another new beginning.

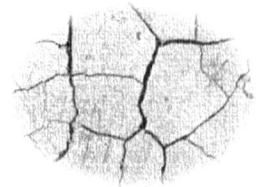

Missing You Wendy

Remembering
the hot lazy summer days.
We'd sit and
talk for hours.
Making plans for the
Wedding day.
White dresses,
painting her nails
and drinking root beer.
How I miss those days.
I wish they'd lasted forever.
Sitting on the back
porch swing, together.

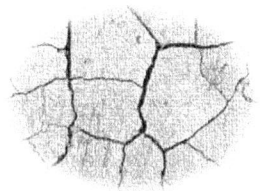

Blue

There definitely are
different shades of Blue.
One of them is
missing you.
The house seems empty
even though
it's a very busy place.
The day seems longer
yet I knew
these days would come.
Wiping tears off my cheeks
Seem normal now during the day.
When little things remind me of you,
like blending
different colours of Blue.

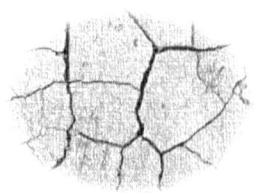

Rhonda, the Salon

It's hard to repay such gifts of love.
Years, I have come here and sat in her chair.
A little clip here and a little clip there.
I watch and wait as they create their master pieces.
Rhonda listens and empathizes while she straightens or teases.
We laugh and we've cried over friends that leave us.
They curl and straighten long hair and short.
They can do any colour of the rainbow you want,
but not mine, I'm not the bravest.
There dryers are blowing and the hot irons are blazing.
People keep coming, it really is amazing.
Oh yes, there's their cat but this is his home.
He is quite the gentleman, greeting everyone kindly.
There's nail painting and ear piercings
and little kids sometimes crying and once in a while even sneezing.
The brooms always moving, the coffee's usually brewing.
How's that! She'd say…
With a twinkle in her eye and as I look in the mirror.
She's done it again, she's made me smile.

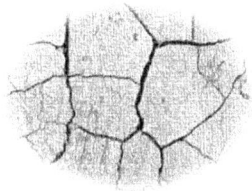

Wendy, My Little Girl

It's just a little past nine
and the piano is silent.
just like my life without you.
My image of you is clear but the room is empty,
her music has slipped away.
Hurts that are so deep
it takes the life out of me.
Lights now lack a glow.
I guess I always thought
I would need to be needed.
It's just me, myself and a piano.
No one here to tickle its keys.
I'm focusing on the hurt and not the healer.
Lord help me to keep that thirst for life.
Navigate me through these deep dark oceans of fear
and anchor me to your
Word of Life.

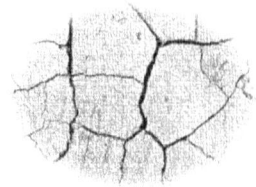

... EVER ...

I love it when
We are happy.
Talk together
Love.
Work together
Show love to
One another
and be one
Together…

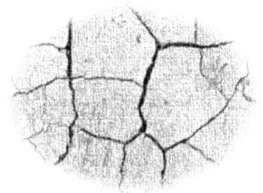

Tracey

It's intriguing to me how God goes with us down so many different roads.
God knows loneliness can wear many different faces.
So the kindness of a stranger is memorable.
Kind people always have room in their hearts for one more.
So we meet, dissolve and barriers, then devote an hour or two.
Morning cups of coffee, essential to the day's progress.
It helps to open the day's doors.
We laugh and share our world of ideas,
and momentarily we're drawn away from the day's pressures.
Our coffee mugs are warm between friends.
It's so nice to understand and be understood; sometimes we just need to cry.
Her life is so busy but she still has time for me.
Tying memories to a cup of coffee.
Slow hot sips, savoring the full gift of her grace and splendor.
Her life is full of music with her hubby Skip, sunny days, and explosions of tenderness
And a happy dog named Eli.
Some smells are remembered for a lifetime, her perfume.
So maybe years down our rocky roads of life
You'll remember me and I'll remember you,
As one of Gods precious gifts,
Neighbours.
Love Wendy.

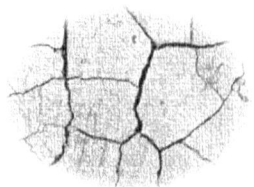

Lois

Loving God and loving others
Just for a moment, let's open our hearts
and think of our mothers and daughters and others.
Life can take away more then it gives.
It's God that will give us waves of mercy and put people in our lives
to help us with life's battles.
To teach us o quiet our souls and to recognize God in this world around us.
Now God has given us a Song Bird,
and with a melody in her heart.
Birds belong in the sky, but this Song Bird is here with us.
With her quietness and confidence in God.
Her soft, elegant whisper
and arms made of tenderness, a loving mother.
Her blue eyes seem to see the hope for the future and the potential in us.
The beauty in her heart blossoms like flowers.
Kind people have room in their heart for one more and they never seem to be
afraid.
I've watched her sometimes on a Sunday mornings as she sits with her Bible
open on her knees.
Her fingers move across the pages like she has touched the past,
It renders me speechless.
Only God knew that she was needed here at Open Bible Baptist Church.
She has wiped the tears off many checks and captured those that have difficultly
trusting
and the souls of broken vessels.
We have come to her with our broken hearts and she's held us with arms of
understanding.
She helps us so we can face tomorrow because our journeys make us weary.
She knows a few things or two about what a mother would do
and she's made some of us laugh till we cried.
She's such a delicate soul and her husband, he gave life to her dreams
and together they have made many bouquets of warm memories, with roots that
run deep.
God's love doesn't fade it consumes us.
Oh, how she inspires me to be the women God intended me to be.
God will cause our love to thrive and his unfailing love will be there forever.
Moments are not given twice.
So I want to take this moment and tell you,
Mrs. Lois Sawatzky, you are well loved.

Freda

I watch the stars twinkle and the night grow even darker,
I reflect on this precious day of sadness.
I laid a rose down on a casket, said 'goodbye' to a lovely woman that I loved as a mother.
Her daughter and I were inseparable friends, schoolmates, we were thirsty for life and had so much fun.
We were a couple of crazy girls riding double on a bike, played tennis, went camping, teased other friends, gave them candies that made their mouth turn blue.
Learned to drive and going for ice cream, our adventures where wondererful, and cartwheels in the back yard.
We went to Spain toured the mountains watched courageous matadors with their swords and spin their red cape fighting with the bull. We danced & laughed, drank wine almost all day everyday of our vacation. Two young women and a dog named Sam.
It was your mom that was there for both of us. I can still see her standing in the kitchen with her apron on and she always asked if I wanted something to eat.
She loved her family, and in that little white house there was love in there and it came from her.
Now here I stand and say goodbye, as memories flood my mind.
Then you said to me, "She loved you, you know."
I looked at you and I could feel my heart warmed and tears start to flow. I loved her also. I knew she was there and she always cared. Years later her arms would hug me as I entered the room.
Now she's gone to her heavenly home above and I know the Lord will look after her.
Her arms will still hold us when we enter Heaven's doors.
Till then we'll wait and let memories warm our hearts and as I stare into the black night and watch the stars, I say to you, "Freda, goodnight sweet lady, goodnight."

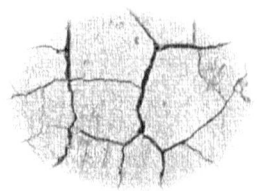

Battles

I can't believe how long I've been saved and have allowed the devil and his evil spirits to suppress my happiness in you, Lord Jesus. I have been so self absorbed. Yes I've had many bad things happen in my life. God has given me many battles but has brought me through each one of them, alive and still standing. I haven't been good at winning the battles. I've wined and cried through all of them, and I've rarely given God the glory for any of my victories. How ashamed I am of my lack of faith and courage and failing to realize over and over again that God is in control he is victorious.

We come into this world with nothing and will go out with nothing. None of us will get out of this alive without Jesus. I was withdrawn and afraid to speak; the devil had darkened my vision. Over shadowed any happiness that the Lord had given me. I was convinced I was a failure. A useless human being hidden behind my shyness. I failed to put on the armor of God. The devil made me feel I couldn't do that, God's armor was too heavy. 'I couldn't do it'. I realized that without bringing God everywhere I went. It is heavy, and you can't do it alone but nothing is impossible for Christ.

The age I've gotten and all the people I've met in my life, never have I went boldly talking to them about you the Lord Jesus Christ. The life giver and sustainer. Forgive me Lord for I have sinned. Souls have been lost because I didn't try. Satan has filled me with fear; I've not relied on you. I thought I could go through life on my own strengths, how foolish I am. We're accountable to you Lord Jesus. Everything is done in vein without you.

Again circumstances in my life have given me further battles and trials. Help me to realize the importance for all Christians to open their mouths and speak of you in boldness without fear. Hope is only in Christ. We're all weak human shells, God limits our time and that's all we have before our battles of life given breath is lost. I know I've not been easy to love but I know God loves me unconditionally.

I have failed but God hasn't. He's been extremely patient with me. Even though we're in Christ we can walk in a maze if we don't follow his leading and direction. Lord keep me focused, I am one of yours. Help me always to see the lost and not material things. Help me not to fear the battles but leave the victories in your capable hands. Our eyes must always be open, its fear that keeps them blind and unwilling.

The House

There is a single candle lit in a house window down the road. Memories flash every time I pass by. A light, cold days, long night's children playing, hopes filled with delight. As I get older some things I've forgotten or I've chosen to forget.
A light, a well lit home. Our lives in this house of windows Mom and Dad built it with little money, tears and sweat. Nine children, lots of work to be done, bills sometimes not paid but stomachs were filled. We did as we were told, tears were shed, our hearts were well hid in that home.
My mother died young, she was the brightest light, now it's gone out. Children crying, people I don't know, hearts broken. Filled ashtrays and a dog that never runs astray. These things came to mind just because of a candle lit at night.
Snowstorms, no mittens, sledding 'till we were soaked right through. Our backyard ice rinks, skates that didn't fit right but neither did our shoes. A dad so demanding and determined to win every fight.
Children now grown, married and gone - our window lights are now out.
The house seems empty, quiet as times, still there's light. Dad still determined to win every fight. Though now years later he's lost a dear Lady friend. The light now dims, for she put joy in his sad heart. He seems weak, he's actually crying, he's lost his dear "Min.".
His mind now wanders. The light is dim. The booze gets stronger but the memories win. He's weak and needs help, he needs us nine. The light, it's there, dad's still determined to fight.
Cold hospital but warm faces, then a young man came in his room. He played his Chello, a lovely instrument to play a melodic lullaby tune. Close your eyes go to sleep, to soothe him on his flight.
He's now struggling. Hearts beating 'till now' I felt that last beat. Dad's light has faded out. Empty house, still standing, windows are bare and the doors now locked tight.
That house down the road it seem so far away, as I walk past this house. The candle lit in the window, you know, it's fading, too, it's really not that bright.

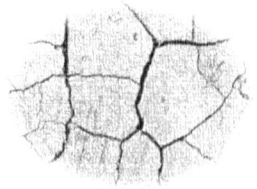

The Nursery

It's Sunday morning and the doors of the Church are open.
God's Word is to be preached.
There's a very special room that most of us forget it is even there.
Parents bring their babies in and that is where the love begins.
Here they come, little boys with suspenders
and little girls with bows in their hair.
Mother's arms release their young babies to the care of a very lovely young lady.
She's there with her tender smile and her stretched out arms
and she says 'come to me', it's so sweet.
When their eyes meet their heart explodes with happiness,
she has a glow of compassion.
The smallest thing can start tears but she seems to quiet their soul
and kiss their tears away.
She has a listening ear while she watches over God's children.
Babies take small uncertain steps but she helps them to realize it's a safe
and comfortable place.
There are times they just fall asleep quickly, she'll watch them while they sleep.
Most days it's just time to play. There are toys and more toys
and stories to be read and lullabies to be sung.
Some want held, some need changed and some need fed
but there is always that one that wants her hand to walk around with them.
Hand in hand and with each wobbly step
they take an exciting journey around the nursery.
How nice to see the innocence of love
and a never ending supply of slobbery kisses and tissues.
Moms know their children are cared for
and their baby's arms will not grow tired of being picked up by her.
You can trace their steps and laughter right back to the nursery
and their they'll be holding hands and singing songs.
With every toy on the floor and with that very lovely young lady,
'Stephanie amidst the messes.'

Carolynn Chloe Belle Mardis

My flower
As dandelion spores float away into the warm Oklahoma sun,I dream, if only for a moment.
As I sit on the front porch swing of my daughter's pale yellow house.
Close my eyes and remember when it was my time to bring home a beautiful baby girl.
God had taken my mom long before I knew what a mother was for.
How fast the years have passed but the wonderful memories have never faded, my legacy.
My babies were hearers of my heart, a language only a mother and a child understand.
Now we've decorated the house with balloons.
A awaiting the arrival of a new baby girl to be welcomed home.
I'm held captive by this beautiful blue eyed baby girl, Carolynn Chloe Belle Mardis.
I reach out to hold this new precious gift.
She lets out a soft sigh and repositioned herself in my arms.
There's laughter, her older siblings are running down the hallway
They want to see their new sister. When I look at my daughter she smiles.
She's now a mother of three, and looking at her I know I did something right.
My time here with them is so short.
The night before I leave, I sit in the same old rocking chair as I did with the other
Children when they too were babies.
That Oklahoma wind is blowing and the moonlight shines across the floor. I rock little Carolynn and she sees me with those big blue eyes, a little part of me that will live in her.
I wish that I could hold her more, my little flower, please remember me. It's not easy letting go of the ones you love. I'm still holding on to my daughter.
I see the tears in my baby's eyes.
I'm drawn in with little Carolynn's blue eyes and her snowy white skin.
I do believe that she had to be born. God wanted the world to see Carolynn's bright smile, a blessing she will be. I'm close even though I'm far away, just like the stars that awaken the senses. Tears and raindrops, love is like a storm but the rain is always needed in Grandma's garden. It's a privilege to have Carolynn Chloe Belle Mardis to my garden. She will bloom and with each new petal of life God will be with her.

Reassurance

The night's stillness has come upon me and my cup of tea has long been cold.
I've looked through my old photograph books and realize
I've forgotten how beautiful I was.
Who knows where time goes?
It's strange the things you remember, moments of lost time faded away,
So unaware of times speed.
I've lived with a thin fail of confidence and missed opportunities.
Does anyone know what I need?
My once wild heart wants to feel the things it used to, so strange.
Life, sensations, fragrances, love and passions only learned through pain.
Sleeping heart awaken my senses, remember me.
I've been blessed with having a child's heart beat on my chest
And years of watching that new life grown and gone.
I love to watch the stars as I sat by the fire
Or be embraced under the moonlight and feel the warmth of my love's skin
and listen to his whispers of love.
In the moonbeams come dance with me.
I want to feel his fingers run down my spine and hold me tight so I feel safe.
Do you think God can see us from beyond the moon "slumbering?
I'm wrestling with my thoughts, Oh how they tease me. I'm better then I was.
That unforgettable first kiss and the dreams of playing in fields of wild flowers,
Making dandelions bracelets and putting flowers in my hair and laugh.
The warmth of the morning sun.
How I love the sounds of the white mourning dove
and long drives to get ice cream and hold hands while we wait.
Missed opportunities. Oh how I need to feel loved again.
Does anyone really know when it is their moment to enjoy life?
Sometimes the last things you want to listen to is silence.
Life doesn't always glitter like gold.
I need reassurance and strong hands to dry my tears.

Passion

My mind is like the ocean full of memories
Waves that crash to the shore and then roll away.
With each ripple of water that comes I'm caught up in passions and swept away.
As we walk close to the shore through the watery bubbles it tickles my feet with each imagination.
How do I recover from knowing you?
The way you smile and the sparkle in your green eyes.
Repetitions like waves of dangerous liberties, will I lose control.
Every moment we have is soon history.
I've made a lot of mistakes in my life and I got lost along the way.
Like the changes of the tide I've paid a high price for my decisions.
Yet still you don't act like it's a burden to know me.
My flimsy paper heart senses unfamiliar passions and strong waves of desires.
You have lovingly given me your heart and you've never made me cry.
Etched in the sand you write our names.
You stretch out your hand to me in the light of the moon and realize you've rescued me.
I'm sure you've felt that in my touch.
You have a romantic soul, soft spoken whispers, they've changed me.
The moon has now followed us home.
As I walk away you softly call my name, do you know what that does to me.
I close my eyes when you kiss me.
How I want that moment and scent of you on my sweater to linger for a while.
Time go easy on me tonight, the winds are changing.
Should you get lonesome?
Just follow the moon.

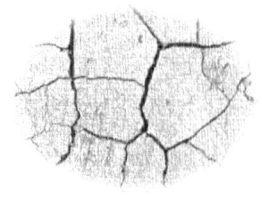

Princess

When I look at you, your eyes remind me that
I could use a friend and a little tenderness.
You look at me, it's intoxicating.
Would you really need a friend like me? Do you actually see me, why?
Love is only in storey books, I'm just a paper doll princess, with a flimsy paper heart.
My heart had to mend. The world is so very small and I fall so easily.
I don't want to pretend. My fears are rooted in my wounds.
It made me quiver though at the thought that you've been thinking of me.
Your voice has a unique echo and then fades away like the morning dew.
You're more than a stranger with kindness.
When I close my eyes to sleep I get lost thinking of your touch.
How sweet the air would be if we were together.
I'll not grow tired of being held by you or feel your breath against my skin.
I'm awakened in the middle of the night and realize, it was just a dream.
Just like a writer without a pen, love needs a partner.
Would you have room for the lonely?
Probably not but thank you for being the reason for making me smile.
As the warm wind blows through my hair and the sun is setting in the distance.
You have said all the right words, so was it me that got it all wrong.
I'll leave my heart's door open as this paper doll princess looks on from her high tower.
I can still see all the carnage of my broken heart.
Waiting for gentle love, Heart to heart talks.
I just can't help but want………..

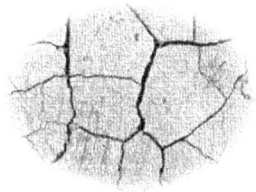

Wild Heart

When I first saw you, you made my head turn and my heart jump.
You were wearing pale blue jeans and a white shirt.
I could feel my body temperature rise.
You were leaning against your shiny Harley Davison motorcycle
in the parking lot.
What a sight and I found it hard to walk past.
You looked up at me in those dark sunglasses, I smiled but we didn't talk.
That warm summer breeze was making me sweat but I think it was the
thought of you.
It didn't matter what I told myself, with you I wanted to break all the rules.
My arms are empty and so were yours and I need someone to hold me.
So let me down gently my wild heart once just wouldn't be enough with him.
Don't take too long to make up your mind; you could be my favorite mistake.
I met him on that beautiful Sunday morning.
I wanted to take you home.
I'm feeling a little sad
And I just can't help but want.
That Harley man.

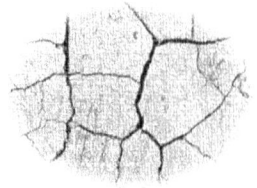

Sassafras Moonbeams

Maybe it is the way you look at me,
I'm just drawn in by you and float away.
It's so hard to turn away from your glance.
It was your touch that
told me you would be easy to love.
I know I could be carried away.
So it's a good thing you can't read my mind.
There we stand in darkness unaware of the world around us,
You just render me speechless.
We struggle through with the moral
Junctions that cross our paths.
I needed you to hold me.
I could hear you breathing and you smelled so delicious.
You were warm as the morning sun and I crumbled in your arms.
Under that sassafras moon, face to face
You kissed me and I wanted more.
My breathing was shallow, stillness overcame me.
We were both so nervous.
I wanted to hang on to that tail from the
Sassafras moonbeam and follow you home.
What could I say after a moment like that?
My eyes are open and I am listening to the silence.
Trying to sooth a new ache inside me I have never known before.
Maybe I'm not what he needs, but he
put joy in my heart. I wanted to laugh,
I was so giddy, like a schoolgirl with a crush.
The memory of our time shared kept me awake that night until I
eventually drifted off to sleep still thinking of you
and trying to catch another moonbeam.

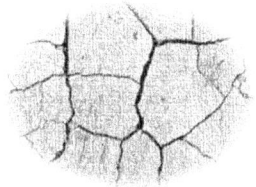

Tomorrow

I cannot know the fullness of your pain
or the oceans of tears that you've cried.
But I do know the love of a mother
and a daughter and the empty arms
that cannot be filled.
God's plans we do not know,
It's a mystery.
You do have the love from many others and
God's knowledge that you'll see her again.
I pray for you and your husband and family.
Tomorrow is not promised to anyone
So today hug the ones you love.

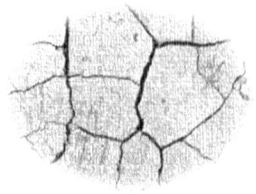

One Tear after Another

Once upon a time, I was pretty with very few worries.
Just like the White Snow Princess, her snowflakes come and stay for a little time.
then one by one they're gone.
Do I have to let you go, I needed you on this Princess's arm. Life can be so unkind.
Am I ever going to be easy on myself?
I just had to leave, I was sitting there thinking of what you had said
and you also letting me read your friend's sad story.
I've heard similar words before but these words that you said to me
"Just want to be friends".
I think that's code for goodbye.
I still can't keep my eyes off of you, you're so handsome.
I guess I'm back to dancing outside in the rain by myself.
At least out there you can't see my tears in the rain
and this princess will need an umbrella not a crown.
Oh my poor run down heart.
Late in the evenings I will look for him on the horizon before the day is done.
Or hope maybe for a knock at my front door.
Maybe I'm just too hard to love or my prince has melted with the snow.
That tone of your voice is echoing in my ears but the pleasures of the flesh are strong.
It's hard to find happiness so I'm back to believing
Happy endings are only in storybooks.
Time ticks on, one tear after another, I could fill the oceans with mine.
……The End…….

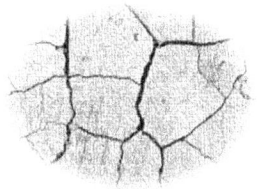

It's only my Poor Heart

The winter is near and that cold wind blows in.
I feel like one of those black starlings balancing on the high wires.
Cold and hanging on for my life.
The sad thing is that there's more like me.
There's one thing about love's road, there's thousands of unseen things, and it's never easy.
I'm so scared of loosing you.
I'll wait, nothing is forgotten. The wind will see me home but I'm alone.
I'm a grown woman, I should know better, but sweet romantic words
Will warm this cold body like an evening fire.
Out of my blue eyes I can picture you and feel your strength, your aura.
It wraps around me and pulls me close to you.
Don't give up on me or throw me away. I know I'm just a storyteller.
I want to read to you but I only write purely fiction.
It's only my poor heart that will be torn apart.
I saw you yesterday and the moonlight kissed your face, I wanted to turn around and call out your name.
You've stirred up my empty heart. I'm losing control my mind and I can't free you from it.
There I've said it, I'm missing you and time has kept me from you.
I want to lay my weary head on your chest, oh my sleepless nights.
There, I can listen to your heart's melody,
It gives me that sweet lullaby, so I can fall sleep.

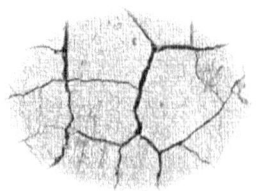

My Knight

I am a broken princess doll and so far away on the island of misfit toys.
It's where my soul has gone, broken and unloved.
Who needs second-hand toys?
Not good enough to be seated beside a handsome prince.
My staff is crooked, my dress is torn, my crown is bent from misuse and my shine is gone.
I've lost my shoes that protect my feet and now my walks are painful.
It's hard to end the day alone.
Many times the sun refuses to shine in my heart, why can't I have happiness?
Someone I could love and die for if I had too.
There are other broken toys, they give me half-hearted smiles, and they know my pain.
There was only one handsome crusader and I gave him my heart.
I think he's stopped looking for me.
He used to say to me, when you can't find me I'll find you, he hasn't rescued me.
I've thrown away his promise with inconsolable tears for he never reached for me to be by his side.
I remember how I felt for him, I adored him.
A life time wouldn't be enough of him.
I'm still waiting for my Knight.
I'll keep on pretending and hold on to those memories.
Tomorrow will soon be the past and it won't matter.
I'm hoping my Knight will still search for me and that he is a true hero
That never dies, especially in my

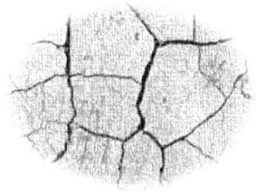

Long Blonde Hair

I've sat in front of my old wooden vanity for years. Looking in that scratched old oval mirror
Combing my long blonde hair. Wishing that mirror could lie to me.
My jewelry box sits on display and visibly I see that pretty little blue box with two gold rings, placed neatly inside. They were on my finger for years.
They're a little tarnished and I can't figure out, what I am saving them for?
I've cried out in the darkness, the shadows on those buttermilk coloured walls, remind me that the heart wounds are deep. How do I free myself from that darkness?
I'm not afraid of looking death in the face, life is much harder.
I'm not brave, I just don't know what to do anymore, I needed a distraction,
I thought it was you, your scent was in my blonde hair. I prayed for someone to be in my life that was true with sweet unknowns and I *would* try to fall in love again
Those green eyes of yours could just make me melt.
I feel like a little girl dressed up in a pretty party dress ready to go to a party but never get there.
Is it only women that cry, I wanted so desperately for you to be real.
I don't want to but I've added you to my sad heart list of people that have hurt me.
Reluctantly my hand slipped away from yours, tears, tears, and tears over flow deep inside me.
I will never push you away and my hearts door is always open but I'm so heartbroken.
I did not want any new lies in my life
with my tear filled eyes, my faith is low, it's like trying to fly into the wind.
I kept a picture of you, I look at your handsome face now and again and think, why would you hurt me?
It eats away at my reasoning. I don't know if I should still love you be mad or embarrassed.
Lord why can't I be in the arms of that man? I adore him.
Oh how I want to feel him against me again, and his lips on mine. I want to retrace my steps
and hear his whispers in my ear and his fingers run down my neck.
How much time must I stay in the valley of loves lost and darkness?
I sit and comb my long blonde hair and wait for that mirror to lie to me again tonight.

Cologne

It's the end of the warm seasons, Autumn is gone and we're passing through a cold snowy winter.
Only then you'll see that silver moon shimmering low in the nights distance.
There you can watch my broken heart dance alone in the evening's glow of the moonbeams.
My body shivers at the thought that I've lost him.
Couldn't his deep blue eyes see that I was needing him?
With my pale blue eyes my world has turned all different shades of blue.
The night mist has blurred my vision and my windows to my world are frosted.
My frozen tears make me cold, and you can see every breath I take.
It's the endlessness that hovers around me like a thick fog.
He still smiles at me but I have to look away. I'm being pulled apart, loves choices.
I want to hold you under winters silver moon. My heart still burns with desire,
The pleasures of the flesh are torturing me.
His touch and his warmth that turns my cheeks to rosy red.
When his lips are on mine how I miss the soft noises he makes when he kisses me
and you know he probably doesn't even know he's doing it.
Not a night goes by my body doesn't yearn for him.
It did my heart good to talk to him even if it was only for just a little while.
The sound of the truth coming from his lips crushed me.
Emptiness in me, spiraling down and your sweet cologne is still lingering in the cold air.
Maybe you're spending time with someone more beautiful, my poor tortured heart teases me.
I can't listen to love songs they truly do make me cry. You can't fix it and I can't help it, loving you.
Evening's cold darkness has stolen you away from me but thank you Lord for the stars.
Distant storms are on the way. The morning light looks much dimmer today.
All through the ages love stories never change, true love is concord, right at the end.
My time will come but not today. Love drifted away with the new fallen winter snow.

Old Records

Standing in my kitchen staring at the empty walls, listening to the facet drip.
The night seemed to go on forever. The clock is ticking. I know God is between the seconds.
There's a place inside my head where I keep things to myself, such an unpleasant darkness.
Wishing sometimes for death, I'd sit alone and watch the car lights swift across the ceiling.
It's so hard to live with secrets, often I wonder what I could have been but wasn't.
Memories keep me pining for lost opportunities.
I don't want to be forever shrouded by clouds of despair, my past wants to haunt my thoughts.
Many times this was not a world I wanted to live in. I know happiness can't be found by looking back.
Then there was you a brown eyed handsome stranger, the world didn't knock the sweetness out of you.
My heart was hurting and our time together is never enough.
I didn't know I even had a shred of trust left in me, glimmers of hope and a gentle touch I didn't know existed.
You seemed to know exactly how I felt. When I looked closer I could see pain.
There's a lot going on behind those eyes of yours. We've discovered similarities.
Come now dance with me and enjoy the musical dreams, timeless steps dancing around the living room.
Listening to those old familiar records spinning. Your arms are tightly holding me and your lips caressing my neck, with your whispers of assurances and hope.
There you quiet my soul so I can recognize you in this dark world around me.
I can tell that you've cried many tears it made me ache inside and I bit my lower lip
just imagining the images of your pain. I'm so sorry if I made you cry or made your mind revisit painful memories. I know those kinds of tears, it's ok to cry.
I do know that where we come from that doesn't make us, we're survivors.
I don't know what lies ahead of us but I do know I want you. Cast your fears aside,
and walk through my front door. An ending worth fighting for, the love of our lives.

Dragons

Oh Lord, who am I?
I've lost sight of my purpose and spent years looking after others but me.
My worlds been torn in two and I shifted my focus, I'm an emotional wreck, lost in time.
I don't know what to do with myself, what have I become? So many endings.
Instead of clutching my weaknesses and fears as always I'm piercing my self esteem.
Fear creeps into me and builds walls, traps me inside myself.
I have to stop chasing the wind. I need to slay my dragons. I need favorable winds and a sword of truth.
I don't won't to wake up one morning and realize youth is gone, where did I go and who are you.
I need to gain control and splash colours of confidence on my broken heart and soul.
How do I forget?
Love has touched me one time, I was looking for happily ever after but I didn't have his heart.
Again, cocooning my emotions because I can't make them go away, I feel real fragile.
I shed more tears because my happiness just can't be found.
I seem to always break down and cry, my thoughts are scattered, like a dropped open bag of marbles.
Where is love leaving me now? I don't want any more tears tonight.
Lord you've taught the rain to fall but my broken heart can't be taught to stop loving him
or remembering his handsome face and deep brown eyes.
He gave life to my dreams but I guess a first kiss should always be earned and happily ever after, should be wanted by both. Such an unpleasant chapter.
There is no ending just a place where you left our story, maybe it's a dream and my prince has fought the dragons. He will come and awaken me with his magical first kiss, but know, I'm a love he left behind.
Cover to cover in my life's story book, unread pages.

Love has many Stories

As I walk the dog alone on this very cold winters night I can see each breath I take in the frosty air.
There is plenty of frost on all the neighbors' windows. But what stands out the most for me in the dark of the night is that single strand of twinkling lights stretched across the front of homes.
Deep inside are my memories, there's a connection to my past with each light aglow.
There are frozen pictures of my family, yet very few are happy moments.
There's some peace within the lights that I've remembered.
Remembering my parents putting their single strand of lights up on their house.
Skating rinks that were made in our backyard. As we giggled for an instant the tick of time relents.
Happiness I seem to have lost somewhere along the way, fun filled days.
Sadly remembering one Christmas with the death of our mother, Christmas wasn't supposed to end that way. So many moments we didn't get to have with her gone.
With each step I take in the drifts of white snow, my footprints disappear as the snow falls all through the night, I wipe my frozen tears off my cheeks.
So many loves lost. Saying goodbye to yesterdays are so hard to do.
God did wave his mercy to me with giving me children, their spouses and grand children to love.
With each ribbon and bow at Christmas, there are numerous happy memories with them.
What my family taught me was love and giving. I want them to remember that no one will ever hold them as tight, as in their mother's arms. My walk is coming to an end on this lovely snowy night.
The dog and I are growing older, no one seems to need me like they did before.
A feeling of a strange warmth has brushed by me like I've been touched by an angel's wing.
Is there music still left in me, like the love that's in the Christmas songs. Just before my eyes close tonight and the lights are turned off, I want my story to end with hope. Call me a dreamer, I know God has knit together my life with his elegance and saved me from so much pain.
Christmas bells will ring on into this cold dark night, awaiting the daylight for the greatest gift ever, Our Lord Jesus Christ.

My Little Girl

Children are the hands by which we take a small hold of heaven
And little girl you have been mine.
The joy, the tears they're my memories to treasure.
I'll hold on to them just like the teardrops I've cried for you.
In your sickness and pain with your dolls and tea pots, frown up dresses and sneakers,
Dandelion bouquets and dirty dishes and always lots of kisses.
Band aids and bothers, fighting with covers and a puppy named princess.
A phone that's always ringing, my little girl is always singing.
Some weekends away, but mom, I miss you! And still lots of kisses.
A boy now a young man, he's asked for her hand.
To love and to cherish in sickness and in health
Till death do you part
And always lots of kisses,
Love mom.

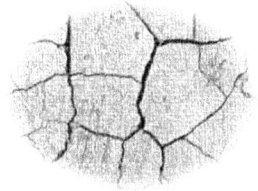

Our Teacher

Our teacher "Make Me A Blessing" Solomon 2;12a
We must always remember that God has given, to every Soul,
Responsibility of deciding,
What its character and destiny shall be.   Charles Jefferson.

Our church, Jesus Christ has dearly blessed this happy place. The little ones, they want to go and not be late for Mrs. Kinsey the Sunday school superintendent she'll be waiting. I'm sure she experiences God's love and our love for her flowing through as blessings, every time we meet. Unforgettable memories that are what she's installed in us; she has found smiles in children where there are none at all.
God's word she teaches, praying with us, encouraging, challenging, to be confident in the word, appreciate one another and when kids begin to fidget there given kind counsel, when it is sorely needed. We learn our lessons and have a special verse; she sparks our interests with the great Bibles stories. It's only a few minutes of a day but it will bring great returns for she is planting the seeds in us.
Being happy cheering on others, having a good laugh, happiness is learned through others. Mrs. Kinsey will laugh with all her children in love; a vital part of their growing up is my favorite sound of Mrs. Kinsey's laughter. It reminds me of how safe and secure we are in the Lord and that I was and am loved. It's important to laugh with others and at our self, to find balance through humor and Mrs. Kinsey is a wonderful example of that. Mrs. Kinsey's deep solid faith in God is encouraging and a blessing to see and to be with. The ability to be happy in the present is a gift, she teaches us to live lives worthy of God.
We are truly blessed because of her, and in our adulthood when we reflect and remember those important to us and those who have been so special in our lives it's you! MRS. KINSEY we love you.

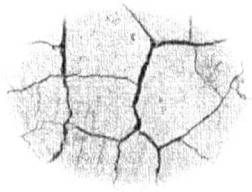

Walk Away

My long blonde hair falls down off my shoulders while sitting at a small table for two. There are shadows that come from a candles glow as he whispers to me soft spoken secrets.
With his entranced expressions on his face, I look into the brown eyes of the man that reminded me I'm alive and full of sensations. At times we dance with the soft piano music playing in the back ground in a dimly lit room. He'll hum that tune quietly in my ear. I want him to tell me I'm beautiful a thousand more times. He's just so charming.
I'm wondering why God sent him across my path - that handsome man could have past by me. I believe you love who you love and there's nothing to be ashamed of, it's so rare. Just the sight of him would drive me crazy and his lingering scent would tease me. Very quickly I needed some explanations, unfortunately a strong shot of honesty.
It was so hard to persuade myself to look away when I still embrace sweet intentions. I have to catch my breath when someone mentions his name. Love's hurt doesn't go away so easy. I wish it could be as simple as some crazy argument coming between us; that's redeemable
There's got to be some place were dreams and hopes don't shatter, maybe another time or place he might have been with me, one of life's altering moments. He's got a life I can't ask him to leave. I guess he shouldn't have ever lied.
Remembering the breath taking scent of the sweet magnolia trees growing out in the country side, in the fresh spring air. It's there such a bold thing I had to say to him then I turned and walked away. I couldn't look back. He took away from me more than his love ever gave. I may not ever get over him. The sadness in my heart hasn't lifted. Sometimes I look at him from across the room and with a broken heart I realize there are galaxy's of unknown stars between us. I know he could never be mine. I still have sweet thoughts of him. He gave life to my dreams. I said I understand but there's that gravitational pull to him, love. I wasn't strong enough to face the truth, look where love has left me now.
Life doesn't give you second chances on the first in your life,
It's disillusionment, true love.

Oh to be

Dear Friend of mine
There's no one like you around. You have such a strong dome-nor
and love for life.
You have loved and lost, you know that life is full of mistakes,
But you stood firm, you took the Lords hand, you sailed through those
stormy seas of life.
You held to Gods anchor, The Word.
You've laughed and cried and we've had so much fun, through your humor.
It's not over yet; there are still rough seas ahead.
Don't look back; keep your eyes looking straight ahead to the Lord.
Continue to be strong even through pain and tears.
There are many behind you with prayers.
So my friend it's late and your light has dimed
I want you to know that I love you.
I'll see you again.

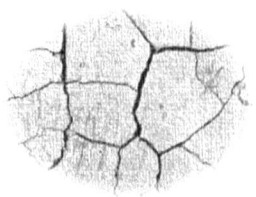

Old Clothes

Mom, we have to be at the hospital at 6:00am tomorrow, we'll call you and let you know what's happening. Well, what do you think a girl or a boy? I still think it's a boy. The next day we waited but of course I was getting impatient and worried so off we went to the hospital. Things were moving slowly, no baby yet, then all of a sudden after a few hands of cards, snacks and drinks in came my son with tears in his eyes, holding a little bundle and full of emotions, it's a boy. I was so happy for both of them.
He's home now and this baby is fussy, reminds me a lot of someone I knew 20 years ago. Just seeing that little boy brought back memories. You didn't realize how much time has gone by till a new baby came in the home. As I was watching the new mom and her baby son it reminded me of a lot of old hurts that I thought were healed.
Mom, we're back from the doctors and our baby is now 10 pounds. No wonder he's growing out of all his clothes already. Suddenly a feeling came over me and I remembered, out in the garage where things were stored, there's a large container I've walked pasted for over 20 years. I struggled to get it down, dirty, dusty and heavy but I did it. Such a strange feeling I was almost nervous. I remember different family members would say to me, 'get rid of all that, it's just old clothes.' I opened the container and there they were. I could hardly believe it they were still in good condition. Little boy's clothes. I brought them in the house and washed them and when they were dry I folded them and held them one by one. The fuzzy blue sleepers I rubbed against my cheek and I began to cry because it occurred to me that these tears were from a long time ago.
Little boy's grow up and move away or sometimes they go home to Jesus. It's taken me a long time to realize that the thing about living in the past is that you forfeit the present. Hey mom, are you home?
We brought the baby for you to see look at his big blue eye and he's smiling'. He fits into all of his daddies old clothes.
Grandma gives lots of hugs and kisses!

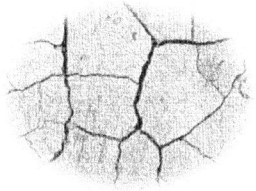

Puppies

Hey mom!
As we're driving down the road, will you talk to me, you're too quiet. Wendy, I'm not, I'm concentrating on my driving. Sure mom, as she continues to do her crossword puzzles with her cute bare feet up on the dash board of the car. Toes pressed against the window, what a sight but happy she is and the wind blowing threw her shining long red hair.
I was really thinking of her, not my driving, such a pretty young girl, thinking as most mothers do. Happy and vibrant such a joy she's added ti my life.
Mom you're quiet again now there must be something wrong. No I'm thinking how cute you are, oh mom don't be so silly. I get it from you she said. We'd drive and she'd sing or she'd talk about everything and nothing, from fingernail polish, too when she needs new shoes for school. My clothes are too small, and this is too tight.
Come on mom you're not saying anything, did you talk to dad, do you think he will be upset? Does he want the new puppy? Do the boys want he too? Wendy, don't worry its fine, let's just see if you like him. We drove up to our friends and her son brought in this little puppy, eight weeks old and eight pounds, a cute bundle of fur. As soon as Wendy seen him I knew we were taking him home. They called him bear but Wendy wasn't so sure, we'll think of something later.
Now Wendy was quiet on the trip home, her thoughts were on puppy. Till she looked at me, do you think dad will like him? I know the boys will. We soon pulled into the driveway and with hesitation she held him. I got out of the car first and dad came to meet us and see. Wendy's door slowly opened then she stood with her head down, 'dad can we keep him?' as she walked over to him.
With a stern look on his face but love in his eyes he said 'the dog must be looked after and trained, he's pretty little you know.' That means yes, thanks dad I must go as she runs with the puppy in her arms. Where? To show my brothers our new puppy.
That poor dog has been hugged and kissed, he is well loved and his new name is now Howard. It's quite the name but I am sure it will grow on us. Just like our little puppy with time.

Mother

I'm here: I've not gone, nor have I faded away.
I'm in the wind that blows threw your hair.
I'm in your touch as you wipe those tears.
When you turn the pages of time of our treasured years.
There, beside you when your dreams come true.
You married, a good man and soon painted baby's room blue.
I'm there when you feel alone, when patience's run low and depression
won't go.
There beside you as you kiss the little ones cheek and hold him so tight
and when you sing him off to sleep.
I was once your mother in the flesh
but now I'm memories.
I'm in your thoughts now and again when you play with him
but most of all
I reflect
Because I'm in you,
My legacy.

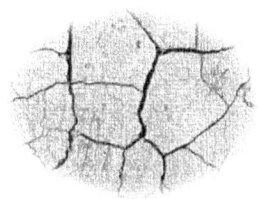

Suntan lines

The warm sun wakes me from the dark; it's far too bright for my sleepy blue eyes. That radio of mine it still keeps playing our song over and over. I find it amazing how some days are so slow, they seem to drag on forever. Yet my years have flown on bye with time. In my youth I remember thinking that I just wasted a whole day and now how I wish I had all of those wasted days back.

Sorrow has rested on my heart and self pity over flows. My life used to be all blue skies but now my favorite colours have all turned to shades of grey in a world of dark shadows.

With rumors, they seem to fly with the wind like the wild hot sporadic embers of a raging gossiping fire. Sometimes there the chances we take when getting close to someone.

Is there any place a sad soul can reside, tell me? Is anyone who they really say that they are? Now there's this sadness that's in me and I don't know where it comes from.

I need time to focus.

Funny, with all the people on the earth why did I fall in love with him? I have no angry words for him. Love never gave me a reason too. How I miss his pursuit and the longing for his scent and the need to touch his face and his suntan lines. I only seemed to have had fragments of his time.

I'm emotionally in pieces now and I feel like I've been left in a maze with no exit.

Am I really acting that strangely? As I stand out in the heat of the day holding my favorite ice-cream cone that I haven't touched and it's melting all down my arm. Without him, today I don't seem to have that much to lose.

Helpless cries and clouds full of tears.

There are definitely shadows still blocking my sunlight.

I couldn't help but fall in love with him, standing together in each other's arms, kissing. My only mistake was not knowing him sooner. I wanted a love that loved every part of me. My world felt almost perfect. Isn't it amazing though how lies are just like sharp arrows that go straight throw each other's hearts? He could have had my whole heart. Will I ever have him in my arms again?

Now the moon with all its romantic notions has saw everything as I now sit alone and watch the sun disappear over the edge of my world.

My fingers they twirl my empty thoughts between the strands of my long blonde hair and I'm watching intently on another wasted day gone on by.

Anne & Bob

Mark 10:9   What therefore God hath joined together, let not man put asunder.

Each breath we take is a gift from God. Love is a treasure and it's come back to us and we have wound up in each other's arms. Yes we've shared a history but enough time has passed as I whisper in her ear sweet romantic words.
Gone are our days of youth but I've never been more certain of anything but our love and time together. The fire has been rekindled and I don't want to count the ticks of time anymore without her. We will step over the threshold of our past and with a lovers whisper and her sweet perfume, she'll see what she truly means to me. As I take her by the hands and I bend down on one knee I've asked her to marry me and spend the rest of our lives together.
Love is just a word till someone comes along and gives it meaning. Now there's a link between her heart and mine. She has chosen to be with me. Her love has made me feel strong. I never thought I would feel that way ever again.
I will try to put the pieces of her heart back together again, softly and be reassuring. No one is ever promised tomorrow but our lives will change today forever. So with her hand in mine we stand together before God and man but so very unaware of the world around us.
God is between our seconds and his Word, our Holy Bible has reminded me that it's the people you love that make you very rich.
There are some moments that define our lives. She has said yes and with our vows share your life with me. So under a thousand stars kiss me with your soft warm lips on mine. True loves kiss with a romantic soul. I will stand by her and no matter what challenges come our way the Lord will take care of us, together.
The silent prayers of our hearts are being heard today. We know our Lord will have us in his hands. Lord lead us, be our shield and protector. We will rest in his Grace.
It's a perfect day for us, we love each other. I softly have spoken and have called her to my side. Before this day has ended she will be my wife and we will be one. Our lives to share and care for, we'll remember this day as the Church wedding bells ring.
Love stories are as old as time but in her heart is where I really want to be. Stepping into today with faith and trusting that no matter how hard yesterday might have been for us. God's mercies will be new everyday for the rest of our lives with a deep, deep peace, our enduring love.

The Lesson

I loved the sunshine warm and bright,
and walked with great delight:
But sometimes on those pleasant days
I wandered far from the wisdom's ways.
And then deep, dark shadows they fell,
For my dear Lord, he loves me.
I know that in the darkness dim,
I'd seek for solace close to him.
In time the shadows go,
I learned to know
It matters not if skies are clear,
But only this, that God is near.

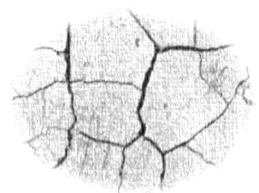

Never Known

I've often felt deep loneliness,
Separated from family.
My body weary from the loneliness.
No one near can comfort.
Passed by from every side.
No one understands or holds out a hand.
Loneliness of tremendous temptation,
misunderstanding when justice is gone,
Mocked and laughed at.
Do some look at me with pity?
No one can solve.
Stand still deaths shadow
I need to focus beyond myself.
God can lift me beyond my despair.
Rejection, suffering and sorrows are mine, not God's.
God is my companionship and purpose
Such Love l have never known before.

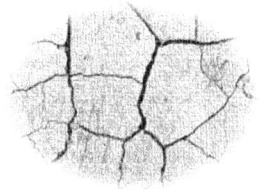

Foresee

With all the time I've spent in love
Yet at night there's no one in the room but me.
The nights last so long. I need to be held while I sleep.
My tears have fallen and touch my lips.
My mended heart can't take back love. You love who you love.
I'm not strong enough to carry such emptiness.
Dandelion puffs they release hopes, for a dreamer.
I'll keep my eyes open, I've needed to see you.
But the one I love loves someone else. I say to myself I understand.
But memories can't just float away like those dandelion spores.
Tears welled up in my blue eyes and I tremble a little.
I think of you often but time is not my companion.
Only for a moment do I want to endure the truth.
Empty dreams are like dew drops
That disappears with the warmth of the morning sun.
Half your love can't please me and you've given away half to another.
How I still taste your soft lips on mine. I sing softly a song just slightly out of tune.
I hesitate for a moment and I look at you, and I think, I shouldn't have been there.
Isn't it always the one you love that hurt you the most?
That hurt I didn't foresee as I sit alone on my knees holding my dandelion bouquet.

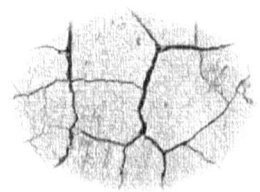

Other books by Wendy Mae Crichton

Special Moments

Children Remember Me

Nearest My Heart

Love, Shadows and Shelters

Stolen Pieces

Visit us online

macdonaldpost.com

dashlegacy.com

www.ingramcontent.com/pod-product-compliance
Lightning Source LLC
Chambersburg PA
CBHW071624040426
42452CB00009B/1468